THE HOLY SPIRIT AND HIS WORK

THE PERSON OF THE HOLY SPIRIT

CAROLINE E. IHUGBA

Copyright © 2011 by Caroline E. Ihugba

The Holy Spirit and His Work
The Person of the Holy Spirit
by Caroline E. Ihugba

Printed in the United States of America

ISBN 9781613790359

All rights reserved solely by the author. The author guarantees all contents are original and do not infringe upon the legal rights of any other person or work. No part of this book may be reproduced in any form without the permission of the author. The views expressed in this book are not necessarily those of the publisher.

Unless otherwise indicated, Bible quotations are taken from The Life Applicable Study Bible, New Living Translation. Copyright © 1996 by Tyndale House Publishers; and The New International Version, (NIV). Copyright © 1973, 1978, 1984 by Zondervan publishing house.

www.xulonpress.com

CONTENT

Introduction

1. Goal and purpose xii
2. Our understanding of the person of
   the Holy Spirit xiii
3. Contempt for the work of the spirit xvi
4. Nature and personality of the Holy Spirit xxi
5. Personal property of the Holy Spirit xxii
6. Understanding or wisdom xxiii
7. Will xxv
8. Power xxvi

Chapter One: Holy Spirit and His work 27
   1. Holy Spirit author of gift 29

  2. The distribution and purpose of gift 30

  3. Abuse of gift 34

  4. Many false claims of the spirit work 34

Chapter Two: Names and Titles of the
Holy Spirit..39

  1. Spirit..40

  2. Spirit of Christ..43

  3. Spirit of God...44

  4. Spirit of Lord God...45

  5. Holy Spirit Holy Ghost 46

  6. Counsellor 48

  7. Comforter...50

  8. Teaching Spirit 52

  9. Spirit of prophecy...53

10. Spirit of Adoption 54

11. Spirit of love..54

12. Spirit of grace..56

Chapter three: Work of the Spirit............................57

1. Holy Spirit in salvation of mankind................59
   - A. Before our conversion while we are yet sinners..59
   - B. In our conversion (New Birth)...................61
   - C. After our conversion for preparation and growth 63
   - D. After our conversion for service................64
   - E. The witness of the Spirit...........................68
   - F. Acceptable worship....................................71

Chapter Four: Baptism with the Holy Spirit..........74

1. Immersion from above 74
2. Baptism in the Holy Spirit 75
3. Definite experience one will know when received...79
4. Biblical example of Spirit filled live 80
5. Evidence of baptism in the Holy Spirit...........83

CONCLUSION...87
About the author 97

PREFACE

In this book, I am going to talk about the life, ministry, work, character, and person of the Holy Spirit. I am going to dig deep into various areas of the Bible to support my facts. The Holy Spirit sets apart Christianity from all other religions of the world. Holy Spirit is mentioned throughout the Bible under different names and titles [(these names and titles will be mentioned later in this discourse with their purpose).]

There have been many series of arguments regarding the identity of the Holy Spirit. Many argue about the status of the person of the Holy Spirit, and ask a lot of questions concerning His identity. They ask, "Is He a person or just a force?" Some claim that the Holy Spirit is merely an impersonal force like gravity or electricity. Others say that He is a strong influence that precedes from God the Father. However, the Scripture presents Him as a real person just as Jesus is a real person. Was He in operation during the Old Testament Era? Is He still in operation today? This is all that I am going to deal with in this discourse.

The word "Holy" means to set apart, to be consecrated and devoted to God. The word "Spirit" means wind or breath. The Holy Spirit existed from eternity. In the old covenant, the Holy Spirit functioned in various ways, such as in the creation, empowering for miracles, healing and in prophetic gifts which foretold of the coming of the Messiah.

HOLY SPIRIT GIVES STRENGTH FOR EXTRAORDINARY TASKS

Judges 3:9-11 says: "when the children of Israel cried out to the Lord, the Lord rose up a deliverer for the children of Israel who delivered them: Othniel the son of Kenaz, Caleb's younger brother. The spirit of the Lord came upon him and he judged Israel. He went out to war and the Lord delivered Cushan- Rishathaim king of Mesopotamia into his hand. And his hand prevailed over Cusham Reshathaim. So the land had rest for forty years then Othniel the son of Kenaz died."

THE HOLY SPIRIT HAS BEEN IN OPERATION BEFORE AND AFTER PENTICOST:

LUKE 1:13-16 "But the Angel said to him: 'Do not be afraid, Zacharais, for your prayer is heard: and your wife Elizabeth will bear you a son, and you shall call his name John. And you will have joy and gladness. And many will rejoice at his birth, for he will be great in the sight of the Lord and shall drink neither wine nor strong drink. He will also be filled with the Holy Spirit even from his mother's womb. And he will turn many of the children of Israel to the Lord their God."

No one can limit the work of the Holy Spirit: he has been in operation before the foundation of the earth.

I pray that the Lord open up your spiritual eyes and understanding as I take you through this journey.

GOAL OF STUDY

The main goal and purpose of this work is for us to understand that the Spirit's work did not end at Pentecost. Some people think that his work ended at Pentecost. It did not; otherwise, all faith in Christ could have ceased, and Christianity also. The Spirit continues to work in the heart of men, convicting of sin, producing repentance and humility, regenerating and sanctifying, supplying grace and helping in prayer.

John 16:8 says, "When he comes he will convict the world of guilt in regard to sin and righteousness and judgement." So the work of the Holy Spirit is ongoing even before the foundation of the world.

OUR UNDERSTANDING OF THE PERSON OF THE HOLY SPIRIT IS LIMITED

"For the things of God knoweth no man, but the spirit of God, and they to whom they are revealed by Him.1 Corinthians 2:11-12" The Bible indicates plainly that there is one supreme, invisible influence by which God did directly control and communicate with the Spirit and mind of the men by which the Bible is written. The invisible influence is the person of the Holy Spirit-God's own very Spirit. (Philippians 2:13)

The natural understanding of the person of the Holy Spirit is insufficient. God, who is the eternal, original spring and fountain of truth, is also the only sovereign cause and author of His revelation to us. The way and means of its communication are suited to the distinct nature of each particular truth. The truth of natural things is made known from God by the exercise of reason, or the due application of the human understanding to the investigation of them: "For the things of a man, knoweth the spirit of man that is in him but as to the supernatural things, the teaching of God is of another nature, and a peculiar application to Him for instruction is required from us." That is why our natural self cannot understand the things of God unless by the Spirit of God. John 3:6-8 says, "That which is born of flesh is flesh, and that which is born of the spirit is spirit, do not marvel as I say to you, 'you must be born again.' The wind blows where it wishes, and you hear the sound of it but you cannot tell where it comes from and where it goes so is everyone who is born of the spirit."

I will explain how the natural man can understand the things of God, when the natural man has believed in the gospel of our Lord Jesus Christ and received him as his Lord and personal saviour, and then Christ will give him the power to become a child of God. That simply means that what is written in John 1:12 has been fulfilled in the life of those that believe. At this point, he becomes a new creature; his/her life and identity will change. He will realize that he cannot do those bad things that he used to do; even though he personally wants to do them, he will realize that he can't. Why? 2 Cor 5:17 says, "therefore, if anyone is in Christ, he is a new creation, the old has gone; the new has come" (NIV). The word of God is real. The power to live for God has been instilled into his life. Those who believe in His name, He gave the power to become children of God. Power to obey God has been given to those who believe. That's why John 14:23 says, "Jesus replied, 'If anyone loves me, he will obey my teachings. My father will love him and we will come to him and make our home with him.'"

You will realize that the character of this individual will begin to change. Why? Just because of the indwelling of the Holy Spirit. Day by day, you will begin to see the character of Christ in the life this believer and that is called 'regeneration', which leads to transformation. Then the person will begin to grow in his relationship with the Lord. All this will only happen with the help of the Holy Spirit. That means that this person is born again, that all that is written in John1:12-13 has taken place in the life of the individual:"Yet to all who receive him, to those who believed in His name, he gave the right to become the children of God - children born not of natural descent, not of human decision or of a husband will, but born of God."

In the second part of this discourse, I will be treating the work of the Holy Spirit in the old creation - in His production, preservation and rule. I have confined myself to expressing testimonies of scripture with such exposition of them as sufficiently evince their own truth. The same may be said of what succeeds concerning His work, under the Old Testament, preparatory for a new creation, in the communication of all sorts of gifts, ordinary and extraordinary, all kinds of skill and abilities in things spiritual, natural, moral, artificial and political.

CONTEMPT FOR THE WORK OF THE SPIRIT

In all the dispensation of God towards His people under the Old Testament, there was nothing of good communicated to them, nothing of worth or excellence wrought in them or by them, but it is expressly assigned to the Holy Spirit as the author and cause of all that happened during the era of the Old Testament. Of all the promise given to them concerning a future and more glorious state of the Church, next to that of the coming of Christ, those are the most eminent which respect a fuller communication of the spirit. In the Old Testament, the same truth of divine inspiration is presented to us in another picture taken from an activity which goes much further back into human history than the contemporary lunge of satellite into space.

Again, we find in the New Testament that whatever concerns the conversion of the elect, the edification of the Church, the sanctification and consolation of believers is so appropriated to Him, which is without His special operation, nothing of it can be enjoyed or performed.

Some critics have taken pains to prove that various things expressly assigned to Him in the gospel, as effects of his power and grace, are only filthy and enthusiasm, or at least, weak imagination of distempered minds. Or is there any end of calumnious imputation of those who avow His work, and profess His grace, but let any person plead for the known work of the spirit of God. They are immediately charged with leaving the rule of the word to attend to revelation and inspiration, as also to forgo all thought of the necessity of the duties of obedience. No work of his is pleaded for but that, without which, no man can attend to the rule of the scripture as he ought, nor perform one duty of obedience in proper manner. That is why the Bible made it very clear in the book of Philippians 2:13, which states that "it is the spirit of God that works both to will and do God's good purpose," for no mortal man can please a holy God with their own wisdom. That is why the book of Isaiah 64:6 states, "all of us have become like one who is unclean, and all our righteous act are like filthy rag: we all shrivel up like a leaf and like a wind our sins sweep us away."

The church, in most ages, has been faced with oppositions, either to the person of the Holy Spirit or

His works; even till today. Yea though the contradictions of some in former ages have been fierce and clamorous, they have fallen short of what is come to pass in our days. For not to mention the Socinians, who have gathered into one head, or rather ulcerous, all the virulent oppositions made to his deity or grace by the Photinians, Macedonians and Pelagians of old; there are others who, professing no enmity to his divine person, admitting the doctrine of the Church concerning it, are yet ready on all occasions to despise his whole work.

A lot of writers have despised the work of the Holy Spirit. What if the whole mystery of the gospel is excluded out of our religion? Take away the dispensation of the Holy Spirit, and its effectual operation in all the intercourse that is between God and men - be ashamed to avow the work attributed to Him in the gospel - and Christianity is plucked out by the roots. Check out the book of the Apostles 9:1ff and the whole of the book of Acts. The Holy Spirit is in charge of the conversion of souls and every other miraculous work. This practical contempt for the work of the Holy Spirit, having become the only plausible defence of religion, is at the same time, the most pernicious, being constantly accompanied with profanes, and commonly issuing in atheism. This is to vindicate the truth and reality of divine spiritual operations in the church – to confess openly what is believed and thought therein concerning the Holy Spirit and His work - to reveal the iniquity of those who are making false and damaging statements against the person of the Holy Spirit and His work. John 8:48 states that "the Jews answered him and said, 'aren't we right in saying that you are a Samaritan and demon-possessed?'" They cannot understand him; neither can they understand what he is saying to them because he is under the influence of the Holy Spirit. Many times, they ask Christ, "Under what authority are you doing this thing?" They cannot understand Him, and then they say that He is demon-possessed.

NATURE AND PERSONALITY OF THE HOLY SPIRIT

Holiness is the central nature or quality of God. I also argue that God relates to us according to His nature through His qualities. Thus, He relates to us through His Holiness, justice, love goodness, truth, mercy, grace and righteousness. Since this is true, it will be wrong to focus just on saying that it represents the nature of the Holy Spirit.

In truth, God's nature is one of Holy love; Romans 5:5 says, "And hope does not disappoint us because God has poured his love into our hearts by the Holy Spirit, whom he has given us." So Holiness describes His purity, moral character and the Excellency of His love. One scholar has noted that divine Holiness requires the Holy Spirit to always act out of pure love and this love seeks always to win His objects to Holiness. As a result, the Holy Spirit desires to impart Holiness in us as He indwells in us, for He will be satisfied only when we are made Holy. 1 Peter 1:16 for it is written: "be holy, because I am holy."

When we have a proper understanding of the nature of the Holy Spirit, we will also have an exalted concept of God and a hatred for sin and its consequences. In addition, that will make us to live in fear of the Lord because of the presence of the Holy Spirit that is inside of us. This does not mean that we fear God, but in view of His Holiness, we represent Him. Philippians 2:12-13 says, "Therefore, my dear friends, as you have always obeyed - not only in my presence, but now much more in my absence - continue to work out your salvation with fear and trembling, for it is God who works in you to will and to act according to His good purpose." The nature of God and that of the Holy Spirit is interwoven and cannot be separated. His nature being of God is the foundation of all true religion and religious worship in the world.

PERSONAL PROPERTY OF THE HOLY SPIRIT

I want to carry you along as I talk about those properties which are distinctly ascribed to the Holy Spirit.

UNDERSTANDING OR WISDOM

The first inseparable property of an intelligent substance is ascribed to the person of the Holy Ghost in the acts and effect of wisdom. In the book of Ephesians 1:17, Apostle Paul was praying for the believers for God to endow them with the spirit of wisdom and understanding (this spirit can only proceed from the Lord), so that they can understand the things of the spirit. "I keep asking that the God of our Lord Jesus Christ the glorious father may give you the spirit of wisdom and revelation so that you may know him better." Every believer desires this spirit. 'The spirit searcheth all things, even the deep things of God" (1 Cor. 2: 10). Now, to search is an act of the understanding, and the Spirit is said to search, because He knoweth; 'no man knoweth the things of man except the man', and likewise, no one knoweth the things of the Spirit except the Spirit. This spirit is wisdom, is knowledge; understand that every believer needs it.

As it is with respect to temporal concern, we know not of ourselves what to pray for. Romans 8:26-27 says, "In the same way, the Spirit helps us in our weaknesses. We do not know what we ought to pray for, but the spirit himself intercedes for us with groans that words cannot express. And he who searches our hearts knows the mind of the spirit, because the spirit intercedes for the saints in accordance to God's will." Whatever sense may be of them, under what conditions and limitations, with what frame of spirit, what submission to the will of God, they are to be made the matter of our prayers, we know not: "For who knoweth not what is good for a man in this life, all the days of his vein life, which he spendeth as a shadow?" (Eccles. 6:12). In this also, we need to be 'taught of God'. The spirit of God alone acquaints us with the grace and mercy prepared for our relief in the promise of God.

WILL

A will is ascribed to Him; and this is the most eminent and distinguishing character of a person. Whatever is imbued with an intelligent will, is a person. Now all this property is ascribed to the person of the Holy Spirit. "All these are the work of one and the same Spirit, and he gives them to each one, just as he determines" (1 Cor. 12: 11). The Holy Spirit's sovereignty determines which gift or gifts each believer should have, showing that the Spirit has a will, mind, knowledge and judgement. Romans 8:27 refers to "the mind of the Spirit" this mind is able to make a judgement and a decision "seem good" to the Holy Spirit (Act 15:28). These verses apply to a distinct intelligence in this discourse on the personality of the Holy Spirit. We can see the Holy Spirit as having personal characteristics: the Spirit has a mind and will, speaks and can be spoken to, and acts and intercedes for us. All these indicate personality in the theological sense. The Holy Spirit is a person or Hypostasis in the same sense that the Father and Son are.

POWER

Another property of a living person is power. A power whereby the Holy Spirit is able to act according to the guidance of His understanding and the determination of His will; this declares Him to be a person. Thus Job speaks, "the Spirit of God has made me, and the breath of the Almighty has given me life" (Job 33:4). Creation is an act of divine power. As He is called the spirit of wisdom and understanding, so He is of might or power (Is. 11:2). We suppose this to mean the effect of His operations, rather than the properties of His nature, yet He who affects wisdom and power in others must first have them in Himself. The spirit will rest on him. The messiah, like David (Is 16:13), will be empowered by the Holy Spirit. The Spirit will endow him with the wisdom to undertake wise purposes and with the power to carry them out.

CHAPTER ONE

THE HOLY SPIRIT AND HIS WORK

Apostle Paul, in 1Corinthian 12, speaks on the exercise of spiritual gifts, which have received abundant measure, and concerning which they have consulted him. For the Lord, having much people in the city of Corinth (Acts18:9-10) whom He intended to call, encouraged the Apostles to go and preach there, and gave great success to their work; He furnished the first converts with such eminent, extraordinary, and miraculous gifts, as might be happily instrumental in the conversion of others.

In the exercise of this gift, several persons had conducted themselves improperly and had abused the gift to the purpose of emulation and ambition. Those among them who are peace-loving and are true to themselves gave this information to Apostle Paul, who wrote to the whole Church concerning this and other occurrences (1Corinthians 12:1) for the purpose of rectifying such abuses. In order to prepare their mind for instruction, realising that they are privileged to be entrusted with the gospel, He reminded them of their state and condition before they were converted to Christ. "You know that you were Gentiles, carried away with dumb idols, even as you were led (V2), hurried with violent impression from the Devil into the service of idols. This he mentioned not to reproach them, but to let them know what frame of mind and what fruit of spirit might be expected of a person, who has received such grace as them."

HOLY SPIRIT- AUTHOR OF GIFT

The Apostles go on to inform the Corinthians that the Spirit is also the author of those gifts, whereby it was to be built up and enlarged. 1Corinthians 12:4 says, "Now there are diversities of gifts but the same spirit," from the Life Applicable Bible. Also, "Now there are different kinds of spiritual gifts, but it is the same Holy spirit who is the source of them all" (V.5). In this verse, the same spirit is called Lord: "there are different kinds of service in the Church, but it is the same Lord we are serving" (V. 6). "There are different ways God works in our lives, but it is the same God who does the work through all of us" (V.7). A spiritual gift is given each of us as a means of helping the entire church. Notwithstanding the diversities of the gift, Apostle Paul made us to understand that it is the same spirit, the same Lord and God, who signifies his sovereign authority in all his operations.

Zondervan NIV study Bible commentary states in 1 Corinthians 12:4-6 that it is the same Spirit, same Lord, and same God. These verses, reflecting the

Trinity, show the diversity and unity of spiritual gift. (V4) Gifts: Gift of grace produced by the indwelling Holy Spirit. (V5) Service: the Greek word in its various forms is used to indicate service to the Christian community, such as serving tables (ACTS 6:2-3); it is also the word used for the office of a deacon. (V6) Working: the Greek word indicates power in operation that produces obvious result. (V7): to each the manifestation is given for the common good. Every member of the body of Christ has been given some spiritual gift that is an evidence of the spirit working in their lives. All the gifts are intended to build up the member of the Christian community (see 1 Peter 4:10-11). They are not to be used for selfish advantage, as some in the Corinthian community apparently were doing.

THE DISTRIBUTION AND PURPOSE OF GIFT

The Apostle mentioned the nine gifts. In 1Corinthians 12:4-12:

[4] There are different kinds of gifts, but the same Spirit distributes them. [5] There are different kinds

of service, but the same Lord. **⁶** There are different kinds of working, but in all of them and in everyone it is the same God at work.

⁷ Now to each one the manifestation of the Spirit is given for the common good. **⁸** To one there is given through the Spirit a message of wisdom, to another a message of knowledge by means of the same Spirit, **⁹** to another faith by the same Spirit, to another gifts of healing by that one Spirit, **¹⁰** to another miraculous powers, to another prophecy, to another distinguishing between spirits, to another speaking in different kinds of tongues,[a] and to still another the interpretation of tongues.

With respect to their general nature, the apostle distributes them into "gifts, administrations, and operations" (V.4-6), and then declares the general end and the design of the spirit, in his communication of them to the Church. "But the manifestation; or revelation of the spirit is given to every man to profit withal" (V.7). That is the gifts whereby he manifests his care of the Church, and his own presence, power, and effectual operations, are granted to some that they may be used for the profit and edification of others. But this is not for secular advantage or honour, nor merely for the spiritual benefits of those who possess them, but for the furtherance of faith and profession in others.

It must be stated that, not everyone has the entire gift or the same kind of gift. Knowledge or wisdom is required to make decisions or to choose the proper course of action.

Faith: (V9) All Christians have faith; some however have the spiritual gift of faith, which is an unusual measure of trust in the power of God.

Prophecy: (V10-11) Prophecy is not just a prediction about the future; it can also mean preaching God's word with power. It can also mean a message imparted to a believer by the Holy Spirit. Distinguishing between spirits: we need the gift of discerment of spirit since there can also be false prophecies that come from evil spirits, this gift is necessary for the church to distinguish the true from the false

Miraculous power: "deeds of power" In the scripture, miracles were events in the eyes of those who experienced and/or witnessed them, clearly evidence of God's power purposefully at work in a way beyond the usual or the expected.

Tongue speaking: Since the Greek word for "tongue" is used to refer to language or dialect, some understand it to refer here as ability to speak human language not learned by other means, as the Apostles did on the day of the Pentecost (Acts 2:4-11). Others believe that "tongues" in 1 Cor 14:9-10 refer to both earthly and heavenly language, including ecstatic languages of praise and prayer.

Interpretation of tongue: The ability to make intelligible the sense of what is spoken in a tongue, so that hearers will understand and be edified (see 1 corinthians13:1, 14:2,10, 14:5, 13, 27-28) This example illustrates the unity and diversity of the different spiritual gifts exercised by God's people, who are all members of one body of Christ.

Apostle Paul goes further to say that the Holy Spirit determines which gift or gifts each believer should have.

THE ABUSE OF THE GIFT

If there be such a diversity of gifts and also differences in their administration, then how can there be unity among the recipient in the exercise of their gifts? It is true that such differences existed in then Corinthian Church whereby one person admires a particular gift and others another gift. Those gifts, which are peculiar to admiration, were preferred over the others and thus led to division and distraction. The division defeats the purpose of the gifts. Due to lack of knowledge to prevent this evil for the future, and to manifest the harmony of this various gifts, the Apostle clarifies any confusion regarding the gift in relation to the Holy Spirit. "It is the one and only Holy Spirit who distribute these gifts. He alone decides which gift each person should have" 1corinthians12:11 (New living study Bible 1996:1821).

MANY FALSE CLAIMS OF THE SPIRIT WORK

The most signal gift of the Spirit under the Old Testament was that of the prophecy. This was deservedly in great reputation, as having the impression of God's authority upon it, and of His nearness to man: In the entire period of Israel's history in the Old Testament, there appear to be no greater gift than the gift of prohecy. The prophets were noble and holy men of God. They were the representative of God to Israel, declaring His word, His mind, and His will to the nation in terms of prosperity and adversity. The Bible narrates the distinct qualities of real or true prophets. The ministry of the prophet is seen to be distinct from the ministry of the priest. The priest was man's representative before God by prayer and sacrifice. The ministry of the priest is from man to God. The prophet, on the other hand, was God's representative to man. He was God's ambassador sent by God with the words of God. In both the Old and New Testament, the Bible said that many people pretended to be prophets because they were looking for recognition. Hence, many pretended to have this gift, but were really motivated by an unclean and lying spirit. But this pretension to the spirit of prophecy casted no contempt on the real gift of the Holy Ghost, but rather increased its lustre;

Peter compares the false prophets under the Old Testament to false teachers under the New: "there were false prophets also among the people, even as there shall be false teachers among you" (2 Pet. 2:1). Based on these points, our brother, Apostle John, gave a caution, because he lived to see a lot of mischief in the Church by this pretence.

Dear friend do not believe every spirit, but test the spirits to see whether they are from God, because many false prophets have gone out into the world. This is how you can recorgnise the spirit of God: every spirit that acknowleges that Jesus Christ has come in the flesh; is from God. (1 John 4:1-2)

False teachers are hereby called false prophets in allusion to the false prophets of old who fabricated their predictions on divine inspirations, but who were really being used by the Devil himself, and sometimes effected "lying miracles" (Matthew 24:24).

The Bible advises us that it is necessary, also, that we have a clear conviction of, and a constant adherence to, some fundamental principles, because if we do not know the principles of the Bible, then we will be deceived. Hence, Paul admonishes in 2 Timothy 2:15:

"Study to show yourself approved to God a work man needed not to be a shame but rightly dividing the word of truth."

False prophets are everywhere, even today, and they have been from old. They easily get at people because they tell them what they want to hear. Jeremiah 29:8-9 says, "Yes this is what the Lord almighty the God of Israel said: do not let the prophets and diviners among you deceive you, do not listen to the dreams you encourage them to have. They are prophesying lies to you in my name. I have not sent them declares the Lord." Let us continue in the teaching of the Lord and search through the scripture day and night so that we will not be deceived, because the Bible said, on the last day, even the very elect will be deceived. I believe this can only happen to those who are searching for miracles instead of the miracle worker himself, who is Jesus. The Bible said those who diligently seek Him will be found by Him. Now He wants to speak to you. Please listen to Him by doing His will, then He will come and abode with you (John 14:23).

CHAPTER TWO

HOLY SPIRIT NAMES AND TITLES

I n this chapter, I will be discussing who the Holy Spirit is, His titles, Nature, baptism and His work. At the end of this chapter, many of the questions that people ask about the person of the Holy Spirit and His works would have been answered.

HOLY SPIRIT NAMES AND TITLES

It is very necessary, before we discuss about the nature, baptism and the work itself, to look at various names given to the person of the Holy Spirit.

Various titles have been given to the person of the Holy Spirit. All these titles will be discussed with their Bible references in this chapter.

SPIRIT

Here, I am going to give a breakdown of who the Holy Spirit is.

The Holy Spirit is God. He is a divine Spirit who has no need for physical things. He has no limits as to space, time or energy. He possesses all power, wisdom and presence; the whole of the Bible from the Old Testament to New Testament attest to this.

There are several Hebrew and Greek words used in the Bible and translated into English as "Spirit". The Hebrew word "ruwach" means "a wind or breath".

The Greek word "Pneuma" is used for the Holy Spirit to mean the "heart or soul…spiritual life". It is generally admitted that the Hebrew and Greek words, translated into Spirit, signify air in motion, such as a breeze, breath, or wind - that which moves and is not seen. These words are applied to the person of the Holy Spirit in both the Old and New Testaments to a great variety and purposes, because of some general idea in which they agree. But there is a little difficulty in discovering their true meaning; their design and circumstances, as to the subject treated of, determines their signification. We can talk about the spirit of God as a singular, and in every way, He is distinct from everything else denoted by that name; Sometimes, He is called the Spirit absolutely; sometimes He is called the Holy Spirit; sometimes the Spirit of God, etc. Our lord gives us the principle idea of the word, in His conversation with Nicodemus: "The wind bloweth where it listeth, and thou hearest the sound thereof, but canst not tell whence it cometh, nor whither it goeth; so is every one that is borne of the spirit "(John 3:8).

His agency in the spiritual world is represented to us by that of the air in the natural. His names signify His nature or essence, as He is pure, spiritual. So it is said of God: 'God is a Spirit' (John 4: 24) – He is of a pure, spiritual, immaterial nature; not confined to place, nor regarding one more than another in His worship, which is the design of the text to evince. As far as I am concerned, the spirit is not given to the Holy Spirit, in the first place; it is an allusion to the air or wind; for this respect, only to His operations, which are resembled by the wind; but His substance or being is chiefly intended by it.

Perhaps it will be said that this name is not peculiar to the third person, but abstractedly contains a description of the divine nature. I grant that the name 'spirit' is not, in the first place, characteristic of the third person, but as it is peculiarly and constantly ascribed to Him, it declares His special manner and order of existence, so that whenever the Holy Spirit is mentioned, His relation to the Father and Son is included, for He is the Spirit of God. Examples of some of the names with Bible references are as follows.

SPIRIT OF CHRIST

According to the Life Application Study Bible commentary, new living translation, Tyndale 1996, the spirit of Christ is another name for the Holy Spirit (1 Peter 1:11) "trying to find out the time and circumstances to which the Spirit of Christ in them was pointing when he predicted the suffering of Christ and the glories that would follow." Before Jesus left His ministry on Earth to return to Heaven, He promised to send the Holy Spirit, the counsellor, to teach, help, and guide His followers (John 14:15-17, 26, 16:7). The Holy Spirit will tell them all about Jesus and will reveal His glory (John 15:26, 16:14). The Old Testament prophets, writing under the Holy Spirit inspiration (2 Peter 1:20; 21), describe the coming of the messiah. The New Testament Apostles, through the inspiration of the same Spirit, preached the crucified and risen Christ.

SPIRIT OF GOD

Pharaoh recognized that Joseph was a man "filled with the spirit of God" (Genesis 41:38). You probably won't interpret dreams for a king, but those who know you should be able to see God in you, through your kind word, merciful arts, and wise advice. Do your relatives, neighbours, and co-workers see you as a person in whom the spirit of God dwells? (Romans 8:11) The Holy Spirit is God's promise or guarantee of eternal life for those who believe in Him. The spirit is within us now by faith, and by faith, we are certain to live with Christ forever (Mathew 3:16, 17). The doctrine of trinity means that God is three persons and yet one in essence. In this passage, all three persons of the trinity were present and active. God the father speaks; God the son is baptized; God the Holy Spirit descends on Jesus. God is one, yet in three persons at the same time. This is one of God's incomprehensible mysteries. Other references are: Mathew 28:19, John15:26, 1 Corinthians 12: 4-13, etc.

SPIRIT OF THE LORD GOD

He is commonly called the Spirit of God and the Spirit of the Lord where He is first mentioned, "The Spirit of God moved on face of the waters" (Genesis 1:2). And I do not doubt that the name Elohim, which includes a plurality in the same nature, is used in the description of creation to intimate the distinction of the divine persons; it represents the unity of the essence of God. Now the Spirit is called the Spirit of God principally as the Son is called the Son of God. "The son of God as He is so called on the account of His eternal generation, the spirit is called the Spirit of God"1 Samuel 10:10, on account of eternal precession, or emanation. He bears His name to distinguish Him from other spirits.

"The Spirit of the lord God is upon Him because the Lord has anointed me to bring good new to the suffering and afflicted. He has sent me to comfort the broken hearted, to announce liberty to captives, and to open the eyes of the blind." - Isaiah 61:1

Jesus applied this verse to Himself in the synagogue at the Nazareth. "Spirit is on me." The statement may refer to Isaiah in a limited sense, but the messianic servant is the main figure intended. See Luke 4:16-20; this verse tells the messiah's ministry of preaching and healing – to meet every human need. He has anointed me, not with literal oil, but with the Holy Spirit (Zondervan Bible commentary).

On the same account, originally, he is called the "spirit of the Son" and the "spirit of Christ": (Gal. 4:6) "Because you are sons, God sent the spirit of His son into our heart, the spirit who calls out 'Abba, Father'."

Spirit of His son, "our new guardian" (V: 2), is identified as the "spirit of God", "spirit of Christ" (Romans 8:2, 9, Ephesians 1:13-14).

HOLY SPIRIT –HOLYGHOST

He is called, by way of eminence, the Holy Spirit. He is called the "Spirit of God", "holiness" (Ps. 51:11, I*sa.63:10-11,* (Rom. 1:4); and this respects His nature in the first place, and not merely His operations. Many times, God is being described by His nature: "Holy", "the Holy one of Israel", "glorious in Holiness"; so is the Spirit called Holy, to denote the eternal, glorious holiness of His nature. Holiness represent God's complete moral perfection. It is the quality that governs His actions and sets the standard for man's attitudes and actions. Holiness also gives us an idea of separation. In relation to God, it means that He is set apart from anyone and anything that is unclean or sinful. "And because of what Christ did, all others who heard the good News about how to be saved, and trusted Christ, were marked as belonging to Christ by the Holy Spirit, who long ago has been promised to all Christians" (Ephesians 1:13 (TLB))

"Don't cause the Holy Spirit sorrow by the way you live. Remember, he is the one who marks you to be present on that day when salvation from sin will be complete." (Ephesians 4:30).

COUNSELLORS

Here, according to His title, he counsels believers when they are in trouble or going through tough moments. This is one of the most important passages about the Holy Spirit. In our relationship with the Lord, love and obedience goes together as faith cannot be separated from obedience (see John 14:15-18, v. 26, 15:26, 16:7-15). It is the gift of the father, besides Jesus; Counsellor or "Helper" or "Advocate" is a legal term, but with a broader meaning than "counsel for a defence" (1John 2:1). It referred to anyone who helps someone in trouble with the law. The Spirit will always stand by a believer as long as they obey the commandment of Christ. In John 14:15, Jesus said, "if you love me, you will obey what I command, and I will ask the father and he will give you another counsellor to be with you forever" You can see that if you do not obey the commandment of Jesus, you cannot have the counsellor which is the spirit of truth.

(V26) Note: both the Father and the Son is involved in sending the Spirit. (15:26)The Spirit will remind you everything I have said to you. This is crucial for the life of the Church.

According to Friederich ET al.1967 theology dictionary of the New Testament, he said that the word translated as "counsellor" in these passages, and other Johannine writings, is Parakletos. (John 14:16) Its essential meaning is debated (Arndt W.F et al 1979 Greek English Lexicon of the New Testament and other early Christian literature Chicago IL). The word originally meant, in the passive sense, "one who is called to someone's aid." Its earliest usage was in a legal context in the court of justice. He is "a legal assistance" "advocate"; He is the professional legal advisor available to every believer. He is the defender of the accused person. The use of counsellor or parakletos for a representative is to be understood in the light of legal assistance in court, the pleading of another's case. And remember, that is exactly what the Holy Spirit is doing for us.

COMFORTER:

2 Corinthians 1:3-7 says:

Praise to God and father of our Lord Jesus Christ, the father of compassion and the God of all comfort, who comfort us in all our troubles, so that we can comfort those in any trouble with the comfort we ourselves have received from God, for just as the suffering of Christ flow over into our lives, so also through Christ our comfort overflows. If we are distressed it is for your comfort and salvation: if we are comforted it is for your comfort, which produces in you patience of the same suffering we suffer. And our hope for you is firm, because we know that just as you share in our suffering so also you share in our comfort.

This comfort can only come to us through the Holy Spirit that the Lord has given to believers to comfort us in all situations and to strengthen us. In John 14:16-18, Jesus said, "I will ask the father, he will give you another counsellor to be with you forever. The spirit of truth, the world cannot accept him, because he neither sees him nor knows him. But you know him for he lives with you and will be in you. I will not leave you as orphans, I will come to you."

You can see that the Lord cares for us; He is concerned about our comfort. That is why He said that He will not leave us as orphans. Orphans are people without parents, people who have no one to comfort them or provide for them or even care for them. Another name for the Holy Spirit is "counsellor" or "comforter". He counsels us in other to comfort us in our situations. We need him throughout our lifetime, for without the spirit of Christ in our lives, there is no comfort and peace, because the world does not have it and cannot offer it to anyone.

SPIRIT OF JUGEMENT

"When the Lord shall have washed away the filth of the daughters of Zion, and shall have purged the blood of Jerusalem from the midst thereof by the Spirit of judgement, and by the spirit of burning:" Isaiah 4:4 (KJV). Here, the spirit of judgement is the spirit of God, which is the Holy Spirit. He judges us when we sin and convict us of our sins and prompt us to confess our sins to God. Then He cleanses us from our sins so that we can again begin a relationship with the father.

In John 16:7-8, Jesus said, "But I tell you the truth it is for your good that I am going away. Unless I go away the counsellor will not come to you. But if I go I will send him to you. When he comes he will convict the world of guilt in regard to sin and righteousness and judgement:"

THE HOLY SPIRIT IS A TEACHING SPIRIT: - John 14: 25-26; 16: 12-14

These Bible references made it very clear that teaching is part of the Holy Spirit's roles, which remain with believers forever.

"These things I have spoken to you, while I am still with you. But the counsellor, the Holy Spirit, whom the Father will send in my name, He will teach you all things, and bring to your remembrance of all that I have said to you" (John 14: 16).

Some writers made some comment concerning the word "all things". They said that it is highly suspicious. They write first that the Spirit will teach you everything that is necessary. They said the teaching is not for your own salvation but specifically for the work of evangelism (Mathew 10:10). These teachings are contrary to what Jesus had thought during His days on earth, having by-passed them for reasons best known to them. It should not be accepted by all believers. "But the anointing which you have received abides in you, and you do not need that anyone teaches you; as the same anointing teaches you concerning all things, and is true and is not a lie, and just as it has taught you, you will abide in Him" (1John 2:27).

SPIRIT OF PROPHECY

"And I fell at His feet to worship Him. And he said unto me, see thou do it not: I am thy fellow servant, and of thy brethren that have the same testimony of Jesus: worship God. For the testimony of

Jesus is the spirit of prophecy" (Revelation 19:10} (KJV)) The same Holy Spirit is called the "Spirit of prophecy" because Jesus said that He will reveal all things to us. He is the indwelling Spirit living within every believer.

SPIRIT OF ADOPTION

"For ye have not received the spirit of bondage again to fear; but ye have received the spirit of adoption, whereby we cry Abba, Father" (Romans 8:15 (KJV)). Once one believes that Jesus is the Son of God, and believes in Him as Our Lord and saviour, a new Spirit is being born into the believer called the "spirit of adoption", which gives him the right to be a child of God.

SPIRIT OF LOVE

God is Love by nature. The book of Romans 5:5 says that God's love has been poured out in our hearts through the Holy Spirit whom He has given to us (Romans 5:5).

Life Applicable Bible Concordance said that the Father and the Son send the Holy Spirit to fill our lives with love and to enable us to live by His power (Acts 1:8) with all His loving care. How can we do less than serve Him completely in love? When the Holy Spirit comes to live in us, love comes to live in us. God is love (1 John 4:8), and when He comes into our lives, He teaches how to love out of a pure heart. I will make references to various part of the Bible. I paraphrase 1 John 4:12: "No one has at any time [yet] seen God. But if we love one another, God abides (lives and remains) in us and His love (that is love which is essentially His) is brought to completion (to its full maturity, runs its full course, is perfected) in us!"

It is the Holy Spirit who purifies our heart, so that we can allow the sincere love of God to flow through us to others, as we are told in 1 Peter 1:22: "Since by your obedience to the truth through the Holy Spirit you have purified your heart for the sincere affection of the brethren, [see that you] love one another fervently from a pure heart." Here, we have to understand that the aim of the Holy Spirit is to get us to the place where the sincere love of God can flow through us.

SPIRIT OF GRACE

"Then I will pour out the Spirit of grace and prayer on all the people of Jerusalem. They will look on Him they pierced and morn for Him as for an only son, and grieved bitterly for Him as for an oldest child who died" (Zachariah 12:10 (TLB)). You can see that this Spirit of grace is the Spirit of the Living God, which is called the Holy Spirit. It is this spirit that can convince them to mourn when they have realised their mistakes, then this same Spirit will convict them and convert them to the Lord. You are saved by grace, not by works. You are healed by grace. We, knowing God and serving God, are by grace. Everything we receive from God is only by His grace.

The titles mentioned above are all the names given to the Holy Spirit at various times.

CHAPTER THREE

WORKS OF THE SPIRIT

The effect of the Holy Spirit could be both seen and heard. Paul describes the works of the Holy Spirit in his own ministry in these words: "My message and my preaching were not with wise and persuasive words but with a demonstration of the spirit power" (1 Cor. 2:4 NIV). I have experienced it myself so I can testify to the work of the Holy Spirit in my life as a believer. The Lord has used me to heal the sick; the crippled have walked, the dead raised, cancer healed, blind see, the demon-possessed set free. These are a lot of miracles, but to mention a few; all is ascribed to the work of the Holy Spirit.

The Holy Spirit can manifest in different ways in the live of believers.But the manifestation of the spirit is given to each one for the profit of all.

Notice the phrases which Paul uses in connection with the Holy Spirit –the "demonstration of the Spirit" and "manifestation of the Spirit." The presence and operation of the Holy Spirit can produce an effect which can be perceived by our physical senses.

The reality is that the Holy Spirit is very active in the lives of human beings today, both the unsaved as well as the saved. Without the presence of the Holy Spirit, mankind has no hope. We are totally dependent upon Him for salvation, wisdom, courage and direction for our lives in a world that appears to have no direction. The wisest person is the person who listens to the small still voice of the Holy Spirit. 1corinthian 12:7" to each one the manifestation of the spirit is given for the common good."

HOLY SPIRIT IN SALVATION OF MANKIND

Before our conversion, while we are yet sinners, there are three things the Holy Spirit does for sinners:

i) Convince man that he is a sinner
ii) Shows the wrath of God to produce Godly fear
iii) Enlighten man to God's salvation plan

The definitive statement of the work of the Holy Spirit comes to us in Jesus' familiar statement: "And when He comes, He will convince the world of sin and of righteousness and of judgement: of sin, because they do not believe me; of righteousness because I go to the father; and you will see me no more; of judgement because the ruler of this world is judged." (John 16:8-11). These words hardly need explanation. But let us examine the manner in which the Holy Spirit works. It is a convicting, a convincing, a reproving, a rebuking, an exposing, and confuting-men of sin, a proving guilty. In the gospel of John, it is very clear that the spirit encounters the whole being of man:

the mind, the heart and the conscience. It is the spirit of God engaging the spirit of man. The end of the Spirit work is a convicting of sin and of righteousness and of a judgement. Convicting of sin leads to a consciousness of the sinfulness, blame worthiness, and damning effects of sin. Convicting of righteousness lays on the conscience the perfect moral standard of God to which one should attain. Convicting of judgement warns of the outpouring of God's wrath upon those who refuse to conform themselves to the likeness of God and who love sin and wickedness.

The Holy Spirit is the inner voice that tells us something is wrong with our life. That inner voice is a blessed gift from God, who loves us enough to show us our error.

Without the knowledge that we are sinners in the court of God, man has no motivation to seek God's salvation. The guilt and fear of being estranged from God is a necessary requisite to our salvation.

The conviction of the Holy Spirit is the beginning of a new life with God.

IN OUR CONVERSION (NEW BIRTH)

Sinful man has no wisdom, power or ability to change his lifestyle or inner evil nature. There is no pill or therapy to correct the problem of sin. When a person responds to the Holy Spirit's conviction, not only does God forgive, He also changes the person. This change is a spiritual experience that is described in the Bible as being "born again".

"Jesus answered, 'Verily, verily; I say unto thee, except a man is born of water and of the Spirit, he cannot enter into the kingdom. That which is born of flesh; and that which is born of the spirit is Spirit" (John 3:5-6 (NIV)).

The Bible uses various terms to identify this spiritual experience. We are taught that the Holy Spirit "quickens" (makes spiritually alive) and that "He quenches our spiritual thirst." The Bible further states that the Holy Spirit "circumcises the heart" and "frees us from sin and spiritual death."

Each of these phrases reminds us that sinful man is dependent upon God's Spirit to free him from the power of sin and to make him "new creatures" in Christ.

"Therefore if any man be in Christ, he is a new creature: old things are passed away, behold all things are become new" (2 Corinthians 5: 17 (KJV)).

The Holy Spirit is the one who produces a power of righteousness to live above sin (Romans 8: 4-5, Galatians 5:5).

He bears witness that we are now God's children (Roman 8:16). And "washes, sanctifies and justifies" us in the eyes of God (1 Corinthians 6:11, Hebrew 9:14, 1 Peter 1:22). Furthermore, He changes us into the "glory of Christ" (11 Corinthians 3:18) and strengthens us to witness, to overcome and to serve God and our fellow man (Romans 8:3).

He frees us from the Old Testament laws and rituals (2 Corinthians 3:13-18) and adds us to God's one true Church, the body of Christ (Ephesians 2:19-22).

AFTER OUR CONVERSION, THE HOLY SPIRIT HELPS US TO GROW

God's Holy Spirit is ever present in the life of every believer. His presence signifies strength, comfort and protection from evil. Jesus promised, "I will pray the Father, and He shall give you another comforter, that He may abide with you forever; even the spirit of truth; whom the world cannot receive, because he seeth Him not, neither knoweth Him: but you know Him; for He dwelleth with you, and shall be in you. I will not leave you comfortless: I will come to you" (John 14:16-18 (KJV)).

The Holy Spirit is present to guide into all truth (John 16:13, Luke 1:15), to mortify the deeds of the flesh (Romans 8:13), and to help in prayer (Romans 8:26-27, Ephesians 2:18. 6:18, John 4:24).

The Spirit encourages by glorifying Jesus and revealing God's blessings (John 16:14-15, Ephesians 1:17-23).

He also imparts love, peace, joy, faith, patience and meekness (Galatians 5:22-25),

And hereby seals the believer as a child of God (11 Corinthians 1:22, Ephesians 1:13, 4:30).

AFTER OUR CONVERSION, THE HOLY SPIRT HEPLS IN OUR MINISTRY

The Holy Spirit is also present within the believers to empower them for God's ministry. Every believer is called to serve and this can only be done effectively with the wisdom and power that come only from God. No education or training can replace the impact of God's spirit. As a way of validating believers for service, the spirit gives certain gifts for the work of ministry.

With my work with the Lord, I can prove to anyone that no education or training can replace the power of the Holy Ghost. We can see that Apostle Paul is a master of the law. He was a "Pharisee of Pharisee." He was a student under Gamaliel at a time. He was clearly a leader of his day in the Law of Moses. Through his letters, we see that Paul had a masterful command of the scripture.

In fact, one of Paul's letters goes into great details. Listen to his credentials in handling the Law:

"Though I might also have confidence in the flesh: If any other man thinketh he hath whereof he might trust in the flesh, I am more: Circumcised the eight day, of the stock of Israel, of the tribe of Benjamin, and Hebrew of the Hebrews; as touch the Law a Pharisee; concerning zeal, persecuting the Church; touching the righteousness which is in the law, blameless. But what things were gain to me, those I counted loss for Christ. Yea doubtless, and I count all things but loss for the Excellency of the knowledge of Christ Jesus my Lord: for whom I have suffered the loss of all things, and do count them but dung, that I may win Christ" (Philippians 3:4-8).

The Bible said that Peter and the rest of the Apostles were not masters of the law; they were fishermen, tax collectors and such. Each had his place and understanding in the gospel. But it was the master of the law - Paul – who preached, time after time, salvation by grace, grace, and grace. This is because he has been there, knowing too well that it is not about training but is all about grace. I can say that was why

Paul was able to stop Peter when he sought to put the Greek converts to Christianity under the law of the Jews, in the matters of circumcision and dietary laws. The Bible said that Peter was wrong:

> But when Peter came to Antioch, I opposed him to his face, because he was to be blamed. For before some came from James, he ate with the Gentiles. But when they came he drew back and separated himself, being afraid of the (Jews) and also the rest of the Jews dissembling with him, so as even Banabas was led away with their dissembling. But when I saw that they did not walk uprightly with the truth of the gospel, I said to Peter before all, "If you being a Jew live like the gentile, and not as the Jews why do you compel the gentiles to Judaize? (Galatians 2:11-14)

How did Paul, who was raised on the law and who was zealous of the law, come to such a complete turnaround in the Christian Church? It is the work of the Holy Spirit!

You can see that Paul spent the vast majority of his ministry dealing with that type of problem. When he was writing to the Church at Colossians, he said:

"Watch that there is not one robbing you through philosophy and empty deceit, according to the tradition of men, according to the elements of this world, and not according to Christ. For in Him dwells all the fullness of Godhead bodily; and having been filled, you are in Him, who is the head of all rule and authority" (Colossians 2:8-10). Paul warns the Church to beware, because otherwise, someone will rob them of the Holy Spirit, who will teach them all things and direct their paths:

Paul went further to encourage the believer in Ephesus that he was praying for them seriously so that they will receive the spirit of Wisdom to know God and His will. "I keep asking that the God of our Lord Jesus Christ, the glorious father, may give you the spirit of wisdom and revelation, so that you may know him better. I pray also that the eyes of your heart may be enlightened in order that you may know the hope to which he called you, the riches of his glorious inheritance in the saints. and his incomparably great power for us who believe. that power is like the working of his mighty strenth" Ephesians 1:17-19

THE WITNESS OF THE SPIRIT

1 John 5:10 says, "He that believeth on the Son of God hath the witness in himself."

The witness of the Holy Spirit in our spirit is highly important, because that is the assurance that we have got the seal to our inheritance.

We have to realize that this is the most essential. Just like you went to university and cameout without your certificate as proof of your degree: Therefore, the witness in our spirit is the most important and blessed part of His work.

Allusion to it is in the word of God. The following is sufficient to prove it a doctrine

Of revelation John 15:26 says, "He (the Spirit) shall testify of me."

Heb 10:15: "whereof the Holy Ghost also is a witness to us".

1 John 5:6: "And it is the Spirit that beareth witness."

Roman 8:16: "The Spirit itself beareth witness with our spirit."

In view of what has been advanced, touching upon the personal character of the spirit, it will be less necessary that we elaborate at length upon His qualification as a witness. Of His perfect competence for this office, there can be no question. It is essential to a competent witness that He should be of sound mind, and capable of judging the facts to which He testifies. In a pre-eminent degree, does this belong to the Holy Spirit? Thus, in the language of prophecy, is he spoken of: "And the Spirit of the Lord shall rest upon him, the spirit of wisdom and understanding, the spirit of counsel and might, the spirit of knowledge and of the fear of the Lord" (Isaiah 11:2). Who will deny that the Spirit, in this respect, is a competent witness to testify of the Lord Jesus to the Church?

You can agree with yourself that He who testifies to a fact should do so from a personal knowledge of the fact which he attests. The Holy Spirit's witness is intimately acquainted with every fact which He relates and with the nature and the truth of the work to which He testifies. His testimony is based on what He knows, and His own experience to the great fact to the truth to which He witnesses. "Eye hath not seen, nor ear heard, neither have entered into the heart of man, the things which God hath prepared for them that love Him. But God has revealed unto us by His spirit: for the scripture searched all things, yea, and the deep things of God." 1 Corinthians 2:9

As a distinct person in the God head, it is impossible that it should be otherwise. He must know all that passes within the hidden recesses of the divine mind. No "depths of God" but He fathoms them; all the design of Jehovah's mind, the counsel of His will, the thought of His heart, the purpose of His grace, and the act of His love, are known to the eternal Spirit.

ACCEPTABLE WORSHIP

Through the Holy Spirit, we can understand the things of God before we can do them according to His directions; the Bible said that he who is joined unto the Lord is one Spirit (1 Corinthians 6.17).

Therefore, if you want to understand worship, you must understand John 4. It is necessary to know that New Testament passage in order to worship:

A special special question is raised: what is the relationship between worship and man's creation?

Just to be a Christian is too small, because there is a much larger issue in view.

According to John 4:24, "God is a spirit: and they that worship him must worship in spirit," God is a spirit. That is why He made man in His image. If we are in the image of God and God is a spirit, then that means that part of us is spirit. Therefore, we have to relate to Him spiritually. That is why John4: 24 said that we must worship God in spirit and in truth.

Thus, the creation of man is important.

If God desires worship, He must form man with a spirit. The creation of man is unlike all the rest creation, Man's constitution has a part that is like God's constitution. If a man has a question about spirit, then worship also entails a question. In 1 Corinthians 6:17, Paul writes: "he that is joined unto the Lord is one spirit." Check this out: if you pour water into water, all is water. You cannot mix water with oil. This means, at our conversion, we are joined with the lord and we become one

Spirit not one body; only spirit can touch God, who is spirit. That little part of us

Called spirit can touch God and touch eternity.

However, if man wants to use his spirit to worship God, then he must live in the spirit.

He must preserve fellowship with God and maintain communication with Him.

I want to draw your attention to the fall of man, for by man's fall there was

A change in the human constitution: What was the consequence of taking the forbidden fruit? Man's will was marred, his feeling became mixed, and his thought and attitude changed. When Adam and Eve sinned, they underwent a change in their very constitution as it had originally been made by God. Before the fall of man, man had a spirit that could touch God. After the fall, the spirit died, sin influenced man's constitution, and thus, man, as it were, became a different being. Based on this fact, man can no longer relate with God, and that was why Christ came, that through our faith in Him, we can be restored back to God and to our original position, so that we can resume our relationship and worship to our God.

CHAPTER FOUR

THE BAPTISM WITH THE HOLY SPIRIT

In my research about the baptism of the Holy Spirit, I found out that over centuries, there has been arousing keen interest and discussions among ever widening circles of Christian churches. Even today, it continues to be a theme of study, of discussion, and quite often, of controversy in almost all sections of Christendom.

IMMERSION FROM ABOVE

The root meaning of the verb "to baptize" is "to cause something to be dipped or immersed". Thus, the phrase "to baptize in the Holy Spirit" suggests that the believer's personality is immersed, surrounded and enveloped, in the presence and power of the Holy Spirit, coming down over him from above and from without.

John the Baptist contrasted his ministry with the ministry of Christ, which was to follow. "I indeed baptise you with water unto {into} repentance, but He who is coming after me is mightier than me, whose sandals I am not worthy to carry. He will baptize you with the Holy Spirit and fire" (Mathew 3:11).

Some groups see it as an experience only of early disciples as recorded in the book of Acts. Others regard it as an essential experience for current believers for the purpose of ministry and service.

BAPTISM IN THE HOLY SPIRIT DEFINED

Notice in the following scriptural references that several terms are used to define the early Church experiences of the Holy Spirit. Let us look at other terminologies used about baptism with the Holy

Spirit, such terms as "baptize with", "filled with", "receive gift of", and "fell fallen upon". All these expressions signify the descent of the Holy Spirit upon the early Christian converts and disciples.

Let us compare the following words. "To baptize" comes from the Greek word "baptizo", which means to make fully wet, overwhelm, and cover wholly. It is used to suggest that the Holy Spirit completely overwhelms a person with His presence.

The word "fills" comes from the Greek word "Pletho", which means to fill, imbue, influence, supply, accomplish, and furnish. It is used to suggest how the Holy Spirit "affects" and empowers a person by His presence.

The suggestion of these two terms is that the baptism (or the infilling) of the Holy Spirit is an overwhelming experience whereby the Holy Spirit ravishes the believer with experience that is available in no other way.

The following is the Word of Jesus to His disciples: "For John truly baptized with water, but ye shall be baptized with the Holy Ghost not many days hence" (Acts 1:5 (KJV)).

"And when the day of Pentecost was fully come, they were all with one accord in one place. And suddenly there came a sound from heaven as of a rushing mighty wind, and it filled the entire house where they were sitting. And there appeared unto them cloven tongues like as of fire, and it sat upon each of them. And they were all filled with the Holy Ghost, and began to speak with other tongues, as the Spirit gave them utterance" (Acts 2:1-4 (KJV)).

The baptism of the Holy Spirit is an experience beyond our spiritual conversion and is available only to those who have surrendered their lives to Christ. Or we can say that "we get the Holy Spirit" when we are born again…but the Holy Spirit gets us when He baptizes us with His overwhelming presence. At this point, the believer has totally surrendered all his or her desires, future and bodies to the leadership and will of God.

Paul's advice is this:

- I beseech you therefore, brethren, by the mercies of God, that ye present your bodies a living sacrifice, holy, acceptable unto God, which is your reasonable service. And be not conformed to this world: but be ye transformed by the renewing of your mind, that ye may prove what is that good, and acceptable, and perfect, will of God. (Romans 12: 1-2 (KJV))

The baptism of the Holy Spirit is a distinct and separate experience from the new birth as we allow God to take total control of our lives.

But now they believe Philip message that Jesus was the messiah and His word concerning the kingdom of God; and many men and women were baptized. Then Simon Himself belief and was baptize and began following Philip where ever he went, and was amazed the miracle he did. When the Apostles back in Jerusalem heard that the people in Samaria had accepted God's message, they send down Peter and John. As soon as they arrived, they began praying for this new Christians to receive the Holy Spirit, for as yet he had not come upon any of them. For they have only be baptized in the name of the Lord Jesus. Then

Peter John laid their hands upon these believers and they received the Holy Spirit. (Acts 8:12-17 (TLB))

DEFINITE EXPERIENCE ONE WILL KNOW WHEN RECEIVED

The baptism of the Holy Spirit is a spiritual experience. It is a onetime experience as the Holy Spirit is permitted total access into the believer's life, and is a continuing experience as the believer allows the Holy Spirit to lead.

Did you receive the Holy Spirit when you believed?" he asked them. "No" they replied, "We don't know what you mean. What is the Holy Spirit? "Then what belief did you acknowledged at your baptism?" he asked. And they replied, "What John the Baptist taught". Then Paul pointed out to them that John Baptism is to demonstrate a desire to turn from sin to God and that those receiving his baptism must then go on to believe in Jesus the one John said would come later. As soon as they heard this, they were baptised in the name of our Lord Jesus. Then when Paul laid his hand upon their heads, the Holy Spirit came on them, and they spoke in other languages and prophesied. (Acts 19:2-6 (TLB))

The main purpose of baptism in the Holy Ghost is for witnessing testimony and service. This is the Word of Jesus to His followers: "But when the Holy Spirit has come upon you, you will receive power to testify about me with great effect, to the people in Jerusalem, throughout Judea, in Samaria, and to the end of the earth, about my death and resurrection" (Acts 1:8 (TLB)).

BIBLICAL EXAMPLES OF {SPIRIT-FILLED} LIVES

"And Jesus being full of the Holy Ghost returned from Jordan and was led by the Spirit into the wilderness" (Luke 4:1 (KJV))

{This is a passage regarding}Jesus' disciples: "And everyone present was filled with the Holy Spirit and began speaking in languages they didn't know, for the Holy Spirit gave them this ability" (Acts 4:8). There are various Biblical references: "But Stephen, full of the Holy Spirit, gazed steadily upward into heaven and saw the glory of God and Jesus standing at God's right hand" (Acts 7:55 (TLB)). When you are filled with the Holy Spirit, the Lord begins to show you mysteries. God will begin to show you hidden things of God through revelations.

The question now to be asked is this: is the baptism with the Holy Spirit still applicable to believers today? The answer is a resounding YES. When we look around at the condition of the present world, evil abounds everywhere. Ungodliness tramples human lives. The professing Christian Church is a mere organization of theological division going through the motion of worship. To the unsaved world, there is little credibility of message or spiritual experience demonstrated by those who profess the name of Christ. Apostle Paul told the believer in Corith that his message was not without the demonstration of the power of God. 1 Corinthians 4:20 says, "For the kingdom of God is not a matter of talk but of power."

Spiritual power has been replaced in the Church by human ideas, culture, planning and production.

The committee replaces prayer meetings with seminars, and the miracle of healing and deliverance is being promoted by a "healing evangelist" who distorts the reality of pure faith. Extremism and emotionalism have replaced the power of God.

The need for a renewed and true infilling of God's Spirit in the lives of today's believers is urgent. The Bible identifies the need for baptism in the Holy Spirit. The book of Revelation describes this era by the prophetic warning to the Laodicean Church: *"I know your deeds that you are neither cold or hot. I wish you were neither hot nor the other! So because you are lukewarm – neither hot or cold- I am about to spit you out of my mouth" (*Revelation 3:15-16). You do not need to tell people that I am a Christian, or a pastor, or Apostle. All these are mere titles. However, there is nothing wrong with them; let the spirit of God in you do the announcement. In 1 Corinthians 2:4-5, Apostle Paul said to the believer in Corinth, "my message and my preaching were not with wise and persuasive word; but with a demonstration of the spirit power; so that your faith might not rest on man's wisdom, but on God's power." The demonstration of God's power through the power of the Holy Spirit is what sets the church apart from every other religion, for Christianity is not a religion, though the world classifies it to be one, but it is a way of life.

EVIDENCE OF BAPTISM IN THE HOLY SPIRIT

The manifestation of speaking with tongues, as the Holy Spirit gives utterance, is the accepted New Testament evidence that a person has received baptism in the Holy Spirit. In confirmation of this conclusion, I may make the following statement.

i. This was the evidence the Apostles themselves received in their own experience.
ii. This was the evidence which the Apostles accepted in the experience of others.
iii. The Apostles never ask for any other alternative evidence.

iv. No other alternative evidence is offered to us anywhere in the New Testament.

There has been a lot of criticism and controversy from different schools of thought, but in this discourse, I am convinced of what the Bible said. That is what I believe and that is what I want every true believer to believe, because the Bible is our yardstick.

Good scriptural evidence is what happened in the house of Cornelius. The scripture says that they were astonished because the gift of the Holy Spirit had been poured out on the gentiles also. For they heard them speak with tongues (Acts 10: 45-46). For Peter and other Jews, the sole and sufficient evidence that the gentiles have received the Holy Spirit was that they spoke in tongues.

In Acts 11, Peter was called to account by the other leaders of the Church in Jerusalem for visiting and preaching to Gentiles. In his own defence, he explained what has taken place in the house of Cornelius. "And as I began to speak, the Holy Spirit falls upon them, as upon us at the beginning" (Acts 11:15).

Here, Apostle Peter was comparing the experience that the household of Cornelius had received with that which the first disciples received on the day of Pentecost. Yet, in the house of Cornelius, there was no mention of a mighty rushing wind or tongues of fire. The one sufficient manifestation, which set the divine seal upon the experience of Cornelius and his household, was that they spoke with tongues. Based on this scriptural evidence, we conclude that the manifestation of speaking with tongues, as the Holy Spirit gives utterance, is the accepted New Testament evidence that a person has received baptism in the Holy Spirit.

CONCLUSION

In this book, I have dealt with who the Holy Spirit is His work, His personality, His purpose and His various names with reference to scripture.

Scripture indicates that the Holy Spirit has divine attributes and works, and is spoken of in the same way as the Father and Son. The Holy Spirit is intelligent, and speaks and acts like a person. This is part of the scriptural evidence that led early Christians to formulate the doctrine of the trinity. There are facts to these based on a survey of some believers; their findings taken from the New Testament are discussed according to three points.

Three points that emerge from this survey of the New Testament data are: (1) the Holy Spirit is everywhere regarded as God; (2) He is God in distinction from the Father and the Son; (3) His deity does not infringe upon the divine unity. In other words, the Holy Spirit is the third person of the triune God. The divine unity cannot be subjected to mathematical ideas of unity. The fourth century theologians learned to speak of three hypostases or persons within the deity, not in the tritheistic sense of three centres of consciousness, but also not in the weaker sense of three economic manifestations.

Although Scripture does not directly say that "the Holy Spirit is God," or that God is triune, these conclusions are based on the scriptural evidence, the Worldwide Church of God teaches that the Holy Spirit is God in the same way that the Father is God and the Son is God.

But when He, the spirit of truth (the truth giving spirit) comes, He will guide you into all the truth (the whole, full truth). For He will not speak His own message {on His own authority}, but He will tell whatever He hears [from the father, He will give the message that has been given to Him], and He will announce and declare to you the things that are to come {that will happen in the future}. (John 16:13)

As we have seen, we Christians serve a triune God, and the Godhead (father, Son, and Holy Spirit) is referred to as the trinity. Usually, when people are missing revelation concerning one of the persons of the Godhead, it is revelation about the Holy Spirit of which they are deprived. Why? Because Satan works very hard to make sure that we don't know what is available to us through the power of the Holy Spirit.

The whole purpose of this book is to help you know who the Holy Spirit is, His power and His work. I have endeavoured to reveal the true nature and ministry of the Holy Spirit.

Of what importance is the Holy Spirit to us as the Disciples of Christ today? If we see the Spirit as a helper without whom it is impossible to have a clear understanding of Jesus and His teaching, then it becomes a necessity for believers to yield their life to the direction of the Holy Spirit.

However, since the Spirit does not perform His role independently, it is very important that the Spirit guides us in a way that is consistent to the teaching of Christ. Moreover, the Spirit does not reveal new things; rather, He enables believers to see the revelation of Christ in a clearer light by unveiling the mysteries that are hidden in the word to believers. The Holy Spirit does not give any revelation that is contrary to that of Christ. Any spirit that gives a revelation that is contrary to that of Christ is anti-Christ in Johannine pneumatology. He warned those who claim to have a new revelation:

Children it is the last hour and as you have heard; that anti Christ is coming, so many anti Christ have come; therefore we know that it is the last hour. (1 John 2:18)

Beloved do not believe every spirit, but test the spirit to see whether they are of God; for many false prophets has gone out into the world. By this you know the spirit of God: every spirit that confesses that Jesus has come in the flesh is of God, and every spirit that does not confess Jesus is not of God. This is the spirit of anti Christ of which you heard that it is coming, and now it is in the world already. (1 John 4:1-3)

Chapter one started with the works of the Holy Spirit, the distribution of gift and the purpose of the gift.

The Holy Spirit is the author of the gift. This chapter deals with gifting and its source. "Now there are diversities but the same spirit" (Life Applicable Bible 1 Corinthians 12:4). "Now there are different kinds of spiritual gifts, but it is the same Holy Spirit who is the source of them all" (V.5). In the same verse, the same spirit is called Lord: "there are different kinds of service in the Church, but it is the same Lord we are serving" (V.6). "There are different ways God works in our lives, but it is the same God who does the work through all of us" (V.7).

A spiritual gift is given each of us as a means of helping the entire Church.

This chapter also deals with the abuse of the gift. If there be such a diversity of gift and also differences in their administration, how would there be unity among the recipient, in the exercise of their gifts? Apostle Paul clarifies any confusion regarding the gift in relation to the Holy Spirit: "It is the one and only Holy Spirit who distribute these gifts. He alone decides which gift each person should have" (V11).

We also deal with many false claims of the spirit work; hence, Apostle Peter compares false prophets under the Old Testament and false teachers under the New Testament: "there were false prophets also among the people, even as there shall be false teachers among you" (2 Peter 2:1). Based on this point, Apostle John gave a caution, because he lived to see a lot of mischief in the Church by this pretence.

"Beloved believes not every spirit, but tries every spirit whether they are God: because many false prophets have gone out into the world. Hereby know we the spirit of God: every spirit that confesses that Jesus have come in the flesh, is of God, and that every spirit that confesses not that Jesus is not come in the flesh is not God." (1John 4:1-2)

As I talk about whom the Holy Spirit is and His various names, titles and personalities. He is a Spirit, the spirit of the living God. He is a divine spirit who has no need for physical things. He has no limit as to space, time or energy. He possesses all power, wisdom and presence.

There are several Hebrew and Greek words used in the Bible and translated into English as "spirit" from the Hebrew word "ruwach", which means a wind or a breath.

The Greek word "pneuma" is used for the Holy Spirit to mean heart or soul, spiritual life. Various names were given to the person of the Holy Spirit. His names signify His nature or essence, as He is pure, spiritual. So it is said of God: "God is a spirit..." (John. 4:24).

He is of a pure, spiritual, immaterial nature, not confirmed to place, nor regarding one more than another in His worship, which is the design of the text to evince. So many names were given to the person of the Holy Spirit, but in this thesis, a few were mentioned, such as the Spirit of Christ (1Peter1:11). He is also known as the Spirit of God (Genesis 41:38). Pharaoh recognized that Joseph was a man "filled with the Spirit of God."

Holy Spirit is the third in God's head. We have God the father, the Son, and the Holy Spirit (Mathew 3:16-17). The doctrine of trinity means that God is three persons and yet one in essence. In this passage, all three persons of the trinity were present and active. God the Father spoke, God the son is baptized, and God the Holy Spirit descended on Jesus. As believers, we must understand this word "trinity" and how the trinity works. Another name given to the person of the Holy Spirit is the Spirit of the Lord (Isaiah 61:1). According to Zandervan Bible commentary, Jesus applied this verse to Himself in the synagogue at Nazareth: the Spirit is on me. This statement may refer to Isaiah in a limited sense, but He, the messianic servant, is the main figure intended. Another name discussed in this book is the Holy Spirit – Holy Ghost. He is called, by way of eminence, the Holy Spirit or the Spirit of God's holiness (Psalm 51:11, Isaiah63:10-11, Romans1:4). This respects His nature in the first place, and not merely His operations. Many times, God is described by His nature: "Holy", "the holy one of Israel", "Glorious in Holiness". So the Spirit is called Holy to designate the eternal glorious holiness of His nature. Holiness represents God's complete moral perfection.

In this book, I also looked at titles that describe what the Holy Spirit does.

Counsellor (John14:15-18) He the Holy Spirit that counsels believers when they are going through tough moments. He is also our helper or advocate. The spirit does a great work in the life of a believer (1John2:1). He is our legal assistance.

Another name that describes what the Holy Spirit does is *comforter (Isaiah*4:4): "the Lord will wash the moral fifth from the women of Jerusalem. He will cleanse Jerusalem of its blood stains by a spirit of judgement that burn like fire" (Life Applicable Bible). Only the Lord can comfort the broken hearted. He will only do all this through the spirit of judgement, which is the Holy Spirit.

The Spirit of Prophecy (Revelation 19:10) (KJV) is the same Holy Spirit, which is called the spirit of prophecy. He is the indwelling spirit living in every believer.

The Holy Spirit is also called the spirit of grace: "then I will pour out the spirit of grace and prayer on all the people of Jerusalem. They will look on Him they pierced and morn as for an only son, and grieved bitterly for Him as for an oldest child who died" Zachariah 12:10 (TLB).

ABOUT THE AUTHOR

Pastor Caroline Ihugba is the founder of New Creation Evangelical mission worldwide and CINDWA, which is Caroline Ihugba's non-denominational widow's association. This association cares for the less privileged widows in Africa. She is among the last set of children to the late Rev David and Caroline Ihugba Igbo, who had over twelve children. She is the last daughter and second-to-the-last, for they are a set of twins.

My father is an Anglican priest who brought the Anglican Church to our village, Orodo Mbaitoli Local Government Owerri Imo State, Nigeria.

Before I had an encounter with the Lord and He sent me forth to go and preach His word and crush the head of the serpent, the Lord had been with me from childhood. God told Jeremiah "Before I formed you in the womb, I knew you before you were born I set you apart; I appointed you as a prophet to the nations." Jeremiah 1:5

I could remember in 1989 after my secondary school, I was travelling from Aba Abia state to Imo state Nigeria in a company of two men. I did not know them; they just gave me a free ride from Aba going to Owerri. As they were talking to themselves about how beautiful I was, suddenly the car somersaulted and that was all I know. Then the Lord opened my eyes to see myself on top of the tree, watching people struggling to put people into the van, including my body that was on the bush because of the accident. That was all the Lord allowed me to see. Then I was not a born again Christian, I was an Anglican and a church goer. Despite my lack of knowledge and zeal, the

Lord was still there for me. Then the next time I regained consciousness was in the hospital, only for me to wake up and I was surprised that I was on a hospital bed with their clothes on. I looked for my bag and shoes but could not see them. I picked up my dress where they had hung it, changed my dress, and as people were sleeping, I left barefooted and went out of the hospital to the road. I entered another free car to our village, as I knew that my mother would be worried, and after that day, I never went back to the hospital or received treatment because of that accident.

As we were growing up, we were taught to pray always; we are made to pray first thing in the morning as we wake up and last thing in the evening before we go to bed. When I finished university and was working, I got an apartment where I was living with my young niece and my young cousin, all about the age of 3-6. We did our morning and evening devotion. This time, the

Lord led me to a living church where I have been baptised by immersion.

One day, as we were doing our morning devotion, my mother was there. Back then, she was still living. The Lord said to me, "Medline will be pregnant." I said to everyone that the Lord had just told me that Medline would be pregnant. So my mother said, "Let me be alive and see Medline have another child." Medline is the wife of my second elder brother, Reginald Igbo. That was the first time I heard the voice of the Lord and a message from Him. During this time, I was not in a seminary; neither was I thinking of becoming a pastor. Within a month, Medline came to the house and I asked her, "Why are you not at the shop with your husband?" She said that she had just missed her period. I asked her, "Have you informed your mother-in-law?" She said no. I told her, "You know how worried she is. Go and tell her." Then I left for work. When I came back, my mother was excited and came to me to tell me that Medline was pregnant. I asked her, "Do you remember when the Lord said this through me and you said let me live to see Medline have another child?" She answered me, "I did not know that you are a prophet." This is because, after her first baby, she tried everything possible to become pregnant, but it was not possible. All her relatives and friends tried everything through every means, but it did not work until the Lord spoke through her servant pastor, Caroline Ihugba, and God confirmed His word. So I do not know what situation you are in, but I advise you to wait upon the Lord, I say wait.

In 1999, in the month of October, the Lord told me to go and tell my mother that she was going to die. Then I left Lagos Nigeria for Imo state Nigeria. Getting home, I told my mother that the Lord said, "You are going to die." Her response was, "There is a woman of God in the village who have already told me, anyway. I am going to join my husband." Then I got back to

Lagos, and prayed and fasted against this, because I loved my mother so much, but to no avail. By the end of December 1999, my mother died. I cried and cried and cried. The Lord said to me, "She is in paradise. Why are you crying?" Then I told everyone to stop crying because mum was in paradise. At this time, I was not very conversant with the Bible, but now I search the scripture every day. I have realised that every word the Lord gave me is in line with scripture. That is when I came to believe that Heaven is real and Hell is real and paradise is real.

In 2000, I came to London with a visiting visa. I was struggling with how to open an account as my document was run out. The Lord told me, "Go to Croydon. I will show you where you will open an account." Then I got up and went to the road to ask someone the way to Croydon. He showed me and told me which bus to take. I entered the bus, not knowing where to go. I slept off in the bus; getting to the last stop, the Lord woke me up and showed me the bank that He had arranged for me. I entered and opened an account. It was like a firm, because the Lord sends me there; He made it possible. I have been everywhere but was not able to open an account even with the help of people who have been in that country for twenty to thirty years. That is why Psalms 108:12b says, "Give us help aid against the enemy for the help of man is worthless" (NIV).

In 2004, the Lord called me and sent me forth to go and preach His word and crush the head of the serpent; that revelation was very clear. That was the first time I saw the Lord clearly and He was with me and collected all the bones in my hand and put them in His pocket. By this time, I was doing my degree in theology. And I have been an associate pastor with New Testament Church where Reverend Andrew Ladipo was a senior pastor. Even in that church, in one of our conventions called "A NIGHT OF REVEJULATION", he invited from Nigeria a politician woman, who pledged to give the church five thousand pounds. And this woman was on crutches. I told the reverend that, as this woman was on crutches and had decided to give us this kind of money, she cannot go back to Nigeria on crutches. The God to whom she has given this money will heal her. And on the day of the convention, after the guest speaker had finished speaking and they had all prayed and danced, I was called out to raise funds for the charity. Already, this woman on crutches had come out to give her five thousand pounds, but when I called out, "Who wants to give one thousand pounds", she came out again. I realised that this was the Holy Spirit who had brought her out. Immediately, she approached the altar. She threw her crutches away and started to run around the hall twice, then she fall at the altar. As I prayed for her, she got up healed. This convention took place on Saturday and she was in church on Sunday without crutches and everyone was pleased with what the Holy Spirit had done through me. This took place in 2003.

The Lord called me in 2004 and told me, "I have removed your seat from New Testament Church. You need to move out." It was very clear. I told my Reverend Andrew Ladipo. It was difficult for him to take in, but that was what the Lord had said, so he had to live by it. In the church it was announced; I was prayed for and sent forth. The Lord did not tell me where to fellowship, so all I did every Sunday was to evangelise from Streatham to Stockwell, and where he led me, I went in fellowship. Until in October 2004, the Lord told me to go and preach His word and crush the head of the serpent, and furthermore, I should register the church. I was thinking on how to register the church as I was praying for direction. The Lord showed me churches that were deformed. Back then, I was doing my degree in theology in South London Christian College. The college was full of pastors. After this revelation, the next day, as I was in the school, Pastor Austen Nana told me to register the church under the assemblies of God, their church. I told him no, because of the deformity in churches that the Lord told me about. Then I started the process and the church was registered in 2005.

Since the inception of this ministry, the Lord had used me to do tremendous miracles: Fred from Uganda was without a kidney for five years, but God restored his kidney after praying for him in 2007; Beatrice Okafor had ceasist on the face. She was supposed to go for operation. As I prayed for her, the ceasist disappeared. She came and gave testimony to this. Blessing Achukwu was diagnosed with breast cancer; as she was about to go for surgery, the Lord prompted her to call me. As I was praying for her, the Lord opened my eyes to see that the demon of cancer had left her body. She was with her husband in the operation room when the surgeon opened up her body. He told her husband that they did not see anything.

A hunchback was removed from Ngozi who had a hunch from when she was five years old, and this hunch was removed when this person was forty-seven years old. Ngozi owulu, a woman who cannot pass air, so that her stomach was so big that people thought she was pregnant, was healed and she came to testify to this. Joy Achukwu, who had been pulling her hair for over ten years, was flown to London from America because of this condition, with no single hair on her head, and as I prayed for her, she was healed with full-grown hair. So much to mention, but a few - the crippled have walked, demon possessed set free, a variety of diseases healed, blind see - I can go on and on. All these people came and testified to this with their medical reports and most of these testimonies are in video. Remember, all these testimonies are the work of the Holy Spirit, which is the evidence of my call, for I have not called myself and cannot accomplish anything outside Christ, for John 15: 5 says, "I am the vine, you are the branches. If a man remains in me and I in him, he will bear much fruit; apart from me you can do nothing" (NIV).

Jesus said in John 14:12, "I tell you the truth, anyone who has faith in me will do what I have been doing. He will do even greater things than these, because I am going to the father."

The Lord said to me, "If they believe, that I am the one who sent you. No matter what needs is theres; I will meet them at the point of their needs." So I don't do the miracle but He who called me and sent me forth told me, if they believe, that He sent me to them. No matter what is their need, He will meet them at the point of their needs. So my message is not with worldly wisdom but the undiluted word of God, as the Lord works alongside the message I preach, confirming the word with signs and wonders. 1 Cor 2:4-5 says, "My message and my preaching were not with wise and persuasive words, but with a demonstration of the spirit power, so that your faith might not rest on men's wisdom, but on God's power."

It is God who does the work through those He has called. Mark 16:20 say, "Then the disciples went out and preached everywhere, and the Lord worked with them and confirmed his word by signs and wonders that accompanied it." I pray that the Holy Spirit will give you insight and understanding as you read on.

www.ingramcontent.com/pod-product-compliance
Lightning Source LLC
LaVergne TN
LVHW041711060526
838201LV00043B/680